The Taxpayer's New Clothes

by Tom TOLES

Foreword by Jeff MacNelly

Andrews, McMeel & Parker
A Universal Press Syndicate Company
Kansas City • New York

ISBN: 0-8362-1256-8
Library of Congress Catalog Card Number: 84-72708

Foreword

This stuff is outrageous.

It's the kind of work that makes your standard editor say, "Hey, this guy can't draw good." Right. Tom Toles does the kind of cartoons that cut right to the guts of the hypocrisy as he sees it. And they are done in delightfully childlike simplicity, befitting the childlike simplicity of the minds of his subjects.

The comic-strip format that Toles uses takes advantage of his masterful timing and comic staging. And now that I've gotten past the part that sounds like one of my old Art History term papers, I'll just tell you that ever since I first saw his graphic goofiness I've been crazy about his cartoons.

It's probably because he's having so much fun at it, and that shines through each of his drawings. But mostly it's the originality. There's something new in Tom's work. He's doing the kind of stuff that most of his colleagues wish they had the guts to do. I'm not talking about content necessarily, but about technique. He's reduced our art form to its bare essentials, and out of it comes stuff that's direct, pure, and most important, great fun.

JEFF MacNELLY
Chicago

ALL YOU NEED TO DEAL WITH THE NEW PHONE SYSTEM

1. THE PHONE BOOK. IT'S OVER 2,000 PAGES, THICK, HEAVY, AND HARD TO READ. YOU'LL GET A NEW ONE EVERY MONTH. IT'S CALLED YOUR PHONE BILL.

2. THE LINES. IF YOUR PHONE BREAKS, IT'S UP TO YOU TO FIGURE OUT IF IT'S THE PHONE OR THE LINES, THEN DETERMINE IF YOU OWN OR RENT YOUR PHONE, WHETHER YOU OWN OR LEASE THE WIRES, WHETHER YOU HAVE TOUCH TONE LINES, ETC.

3. THE RADIATOR PIPE NEAR THE CEILING.

4.

January 5, 1984

January 9, 1984

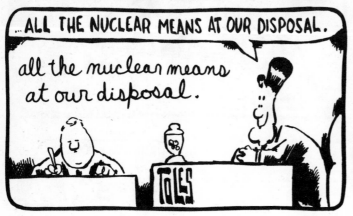

8

January 11, 1984

January 13, 1984

9

10

The New Civil Rights Commission Members Select Their Seats on the Bus

WAITING FOR AN ACID RAIN SOLUTION: THE AMERICAN WATER TORTURE

January 23, 1984

The Survivalist

Today, I re-emerge.

It was 3 long years ago we heard the sirens and holed up down here.

It's been hell. Not enough food, fighting with my companions, having to kill my companions, having to eat my companions... But I survived.

And today I re-emerge.

TOLES

FALSE ALARM.

WELL, THERE'S ALWAYS NEXT TIME...

January 26, 1984

13

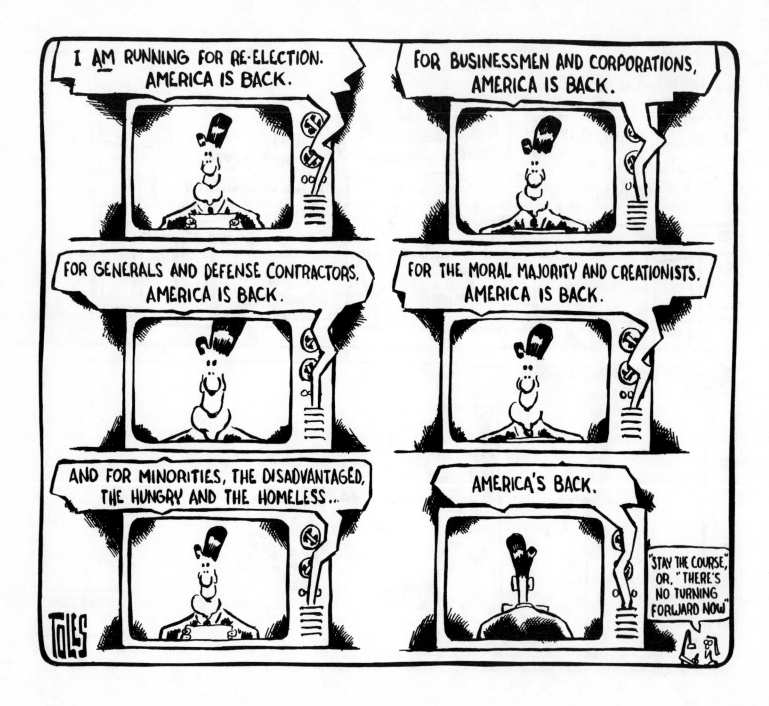

January 31, 1984

February 2, 1984

18

February 7, 1984

19

February 22, 1984

21

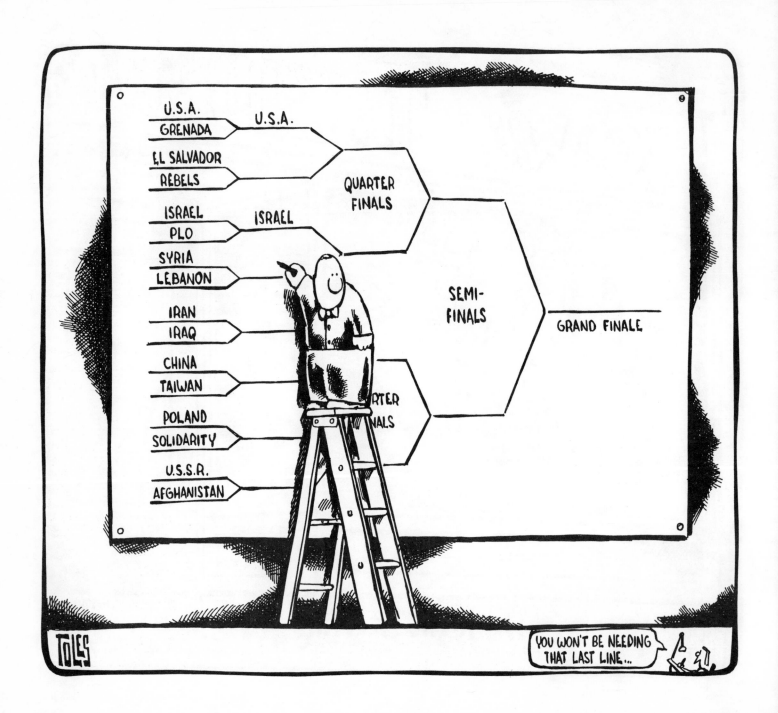

WASHINGTON, D.C.

LAND OF IMPORTANT DECISIONS.

WHERE THE THREAT OF ECONOMIC COLLAPSE FROM RUNAWAY DEFICITS MUST BE FACED.

WHERE QUESTIONS OF HUNGER, POVERTY, AND SOCIAL JUSTICE MUST BE CONFRONTED.

WHERE THE DANGERS OF NUCLEAR ANNIHILATION AND OTHER LIFE AND DEATH PROBLEMS MUST BE HANDLED WITH WISDOM AND SANITY.

WE NEED VOCAL PRAYERS IN SCHOOL..

NO WE DON'T..

OH YES WE DO...

NOW I LAY YOU DOWN TO SLEEP...

March 9, 1984

PUZZLE TIME

TODAY'S PUZZLE: COMPLETE THE PICTURE OF A PEACEFUL, PROSPEROUS CENTRAL AMERICA...

24

Understanding the Hart Phenomenon

March 13, 1984

A TELEVISION EXECUTION

March 14, 1984

How Primary Voting Works

VOTER (A) ENTERS VOTING BOOTH (B)

RUNS INTO MEDIA (C) CONDUCTING PRE-EXIT POLLING, AND CONSULTING THE MOMENTUM GAUGE (D) AND THE WHICH-WAY-ARE-YOU-LEANING METER (E)

ASKED ABOUT HIS PERCEPTIONS, VOTER SEES LIGHT BULB (F) AND MISTAKES IT FOR A NEW IDEA.

VOTER PULLS LEVER (G) TO VOTE FOR LIGHT BULB, BUT TURNS THE LIGHT OUT INSTEAD.

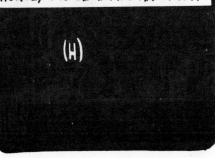

VOTER FINDS HIMSELF IN THE DARK (H), AS USUAL, AND CASTS HIS VOTE. THE MEDIA, ALSO IN THE DARK AS USUAL, HEARS A NOISE, THINKS MAYBE IT'S A DARK HORSE, AND DECLARES AN UPSET.

28

March 20, 1984

FURTHER ADVENTURES OF
CAPTAIN RAY-GUN

AND HIS STAR WARS DEFENSE

WE FIND OUR HERO CRUISING THE HEAVENS SEARCHING FOR BALLISTIC MISSILES TO KNOCK DOWN WITH HIS PARTICLE-BOARD BEAM.

...WHEN SUDDENLY...

EARTH TO CAPTAIN RAY-GUN

RED ALERT. INCOMING REALITY.

IT WAS THE SCIENTISTS. TRYING TO SHOOT DOWN HIS SPACE DEFENSE PROGRAM AGAIN.

IT WON'T WORK.

IT WILL WASTE $26 BILLION.

IT WILL UNDERMINE THE ABM TREATY.

IT WILL CAUSE NEW ESCALATION.

THE CAPTAIN TRIED VALIANTLY TO FEND OFF THE ATTACKS WITH HIS BEAM, BUT IT WAS USELESS AGAINST LOGIC.

ABM TREATY

WON'T WORK

BOUNCE

$26 BILLION

ESCALATION

BUT THEY DIDN'T CALL HIM THE GREAT CARTOON BALLOONICATOR FOR NOTHING. HE HAD A SECRET WEAPON.

THERE YOU GO AGAIN.

A WEAPON OF DEVASTATING POTENTIAL. IN THE RIGHT HANDS, IT COULD PUNCTURE THE MOST COMPELLING ARGUMENTS.

WON'T WORK

THERE YOU GO AGAIN

$26 BILLION.

POP

SKILLFULLY AVOIDING THE POINTS OF THE ENEMY BALLOONS, HE POPPED THEM ALL IN NO TIME.

WON'T WORK

BANG

THERE YOU GO AGAIN

MISSION ACCOMPLISHED. TIME TO RELAX. BUT THERE ARE STILL GREATER CHALLENGES AHEAD.

WHERE UP HERE DO YOU FIND FIREWOOD TO CHOP?

TOLES

TO BE CONTINUED. START SAVING UP YOUR $26 BILLION.

March 23, 1984

29

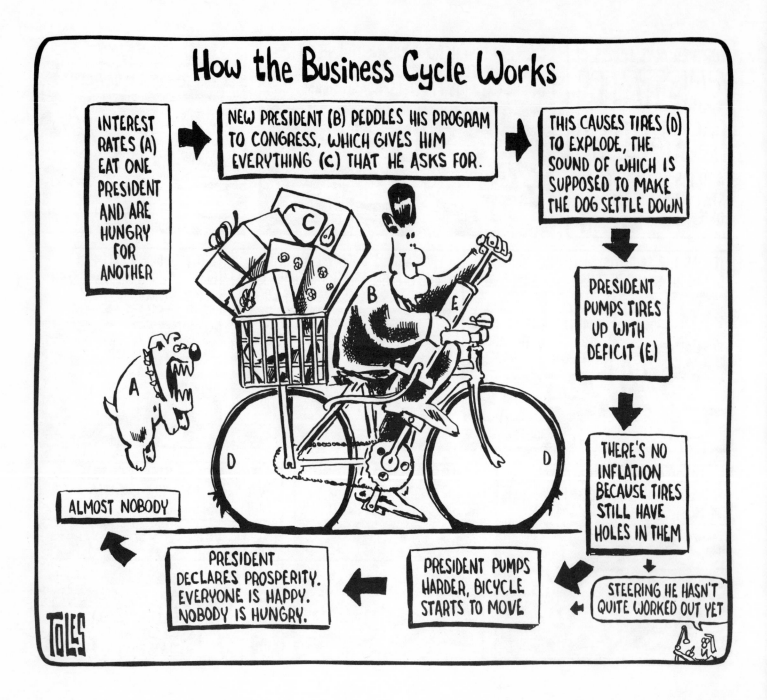

March 27, 1984

Lover's Leap

April 5, 1984

34

April 19, 1984

April 20, 1984

High Noon in Texas

April 25, 1984

(NOTE: PANEL 1 IS IMITATION CHINESE)

April 26, 1984

38

FRONT ROW: OFFICIAL OLYMPIC CARS, POSTERS, SANDWICHES, KEY CHAINS, UNDERSHORTS, MEDIA, HOT DOGS.
MIDDLE ROW: OFFICIAL OLYMPIC OVEN CLEANER, PIPE CLEANER, TOILET CLEANER, PANCAKE MIX, BUG SPRAY.
TOP ROW: OFFICIAL OLYMPIC COINS, MEDALLIONS, GOLD BARS, WRENCHES, LAWN FERTILIZER, PEAS, PANTY HOSE.
BACK ROW: OFFICIAL OLYMPIC ATHLETE.
WORD BALLOON: OFFICIAL OLYMPIC BALONEY.

40

May 14, 1984

41

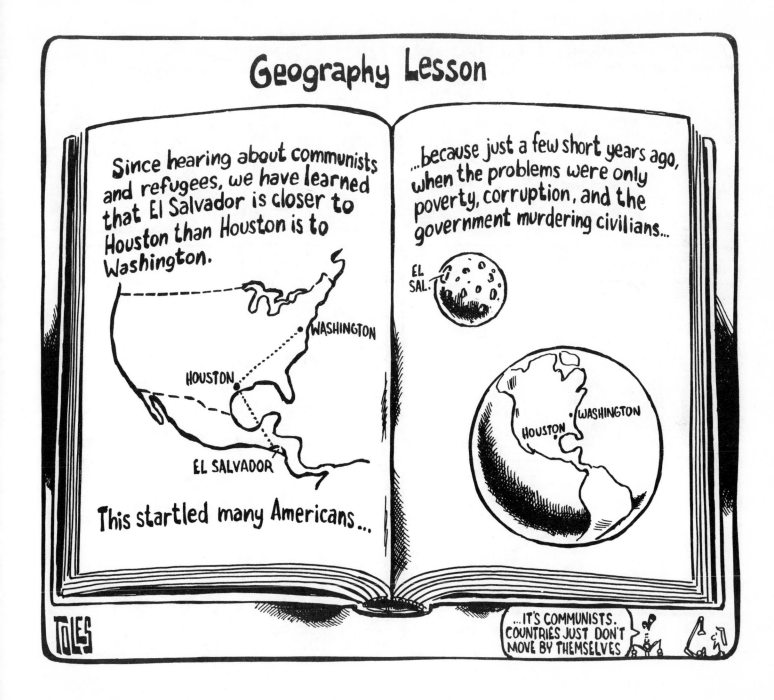

Geography Lesson

Since hearing about communists and refugees, we have learned that El Salvador is closer to Houston than Houston is to Washington.

This startled many Americans...

WASHINGTON

HOUSTON

EL SALVADOR

...because just a few short years ago, when the problems were only poverty, corruption, and the government murdering civilians...

EL SAL.

HOUSTON WASHINGTON

...IT'S COMMUNISTS. COUNTRIES JUST DON'T MOVE BY THEMSELVES

TOLES

May 23, 1984

June 1, 1984

46

June 4, 1984

June 5, 1984

Persian Golf

Water Hazard

Bunker

Birdies

Sand Trap

Teed Off

Pin

The Mondale-Hart Breakfast

July 17, 1984

How the Airbag Works

July 18, 1984

July 19, 1984

The Secret Life of Walter Mondale

DESPITE ALL THE PREDICTIONS, MONDALE WINS THE 1984 PRESIDENTIAL ELECTION.

WINNING SO BIG IN CALIFORNIA WAS THE BEST PART OF ALL.

MONDALE WINS

THE LAST FEW MONTHS ON THE CAMPAIGN TRAIL HAD MADE QUITE A SPEAKER OF MR. MONDALE. HIS INAUGURAL ADDRESS WAS A BIG HIT.

FAR BETTER THAN CUOMO.

THINGS GOT OFF TO A GOOD START. CONGRESS APOLOGIZED FOR GIVING PRESIDENTS TROUBLE IN THE PAST AND PROMISED TO GO ALONG WITH WHATEVER HE THOUGHT BEST.

UNCOVERING THE HUNDREDS OF BILLIONS THAT REAGAN HID IN A SECRET PERSONAL BANK ACCOUNT ENABLED MONDALE TO BALANCE THE BUDGET WITHOUT PAIN TO ANYBODY.

BUDGET

KONSTANTIN CHERNENKO CAME TO THE WHITE HOUSE PERSONALLY TO OFFER A BIG ARMS CONCESSION.

I AM PREPARED NOW TO OFFER YOU A BIG RUBBER WORM.

WHAT?

TOLES

I SAID WOULD YOU LIKE A RUBBER WORM. FOR YOUR HOOK. I'LL PUT IT ON FOR YOU. YOU'VE GOT A LONG CAMPAIGN AHEAD OF YOU...

"I'LL PUT IT ON FOR YOU," HE SAID OF MONDALE'S FIRST NOBEL PEACE PRIZE...

July 25, 1984

July 26, 1984

July 27, 1984

64

August 2, 1984

MONDALE
REAGAN
MONDALE - FER
REAGAN - BU
MONDALE - FERRARO
REAGAN - BU
MONDALE - FERRARO
REAGAN - BURFORD
TOLES
ANOTHER NOTHING-BURGER!

Other Events

At the World Population Conference

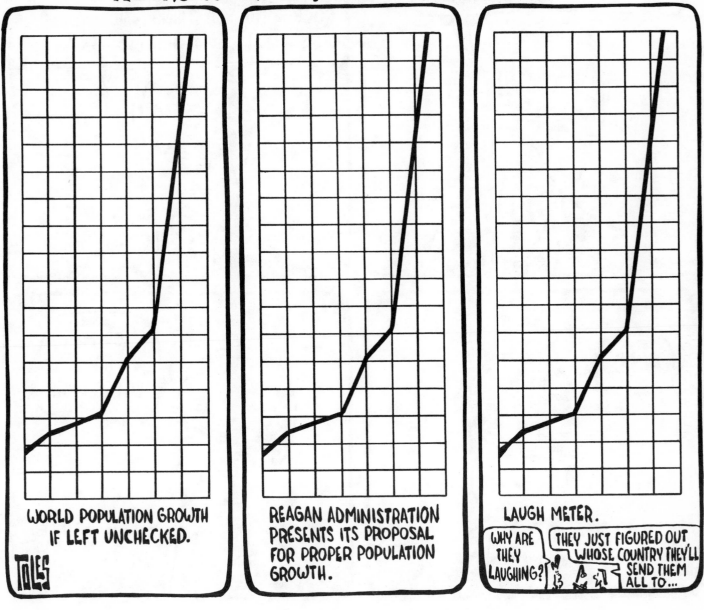

WORLD POPULATION GROWTH IF LEFT UNCHECKED.

REAGAN ADMINISTRATION PRESENTS ITS PROPOSAL FOR PROPER POPULATION GROWTH.

LAUGH METER.

WHY ARE THEY LAUGHING?

THEY JUST FIGURED OUT WHOSE COUNTRY THEY'LL SEND THEM ALL TO...

TOLES

August 9, 1984

August 10, 1984

August 11, 1984

August 15, 1984

August 16, 1984

August 22, 1984

August 29, 1984

August 30, 1984

80

August 31, 1984

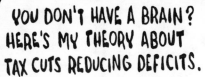

September 5, 1984

81

82

September 11, 1984

83

84

September 12, 1984

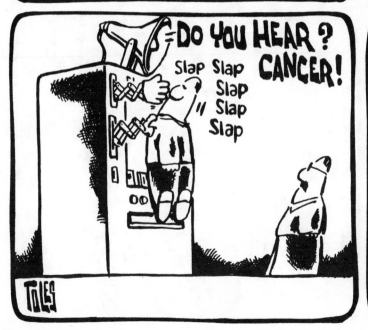

September 13, 1984

86

The Teflon Candidate

The Velcro Candidate

September 21, 1984

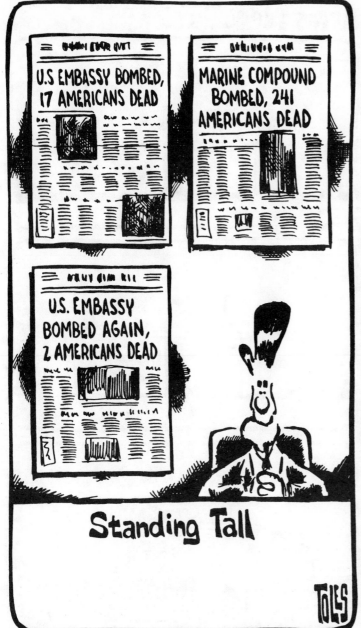

Setting Up for New Arms Negotiations

September 26, 1984

Another Episode of General's Hospital

September 27, 1984

The Tortoise and the Hair

92

94

October 2, 1984

October 3, 1984

The Feeling-Better-About-America Kit

Presidential Debates... Then & Now

October 9, 1984

And now... Barbara Bush

October 15, 1984

October 16, 1984

102

104

Closing Statement

ONE DAY SEVERAL YEARS AGO I WAS DRIVING DOWN THE HIGHWAY.

I WAS THINKING ABOUT A LETTER I WAS GOING TO WRITE TO PEOPLE LIVING A HUNDRED YEARS FROM NOW, AND I WONDERED IF THEY WOULD BE DRIVING DOWN THAT SAME HIGHWAY.

WOULD IT BE THE SAME HIGHWAY OR A DIFFERENT ONE? AND WOULD THEY SEE THE SAME THINGS OR DIFFERENT THINGS? AND I WONDERED WHAT KIND OF CAR THEY'D BE DRIVING AND WHAT THEY WOULD BE WEARING.

THEY WOULD KNOW ABOUT OUR NUCLEAR WEAPONS AND WHETHER WE HAD USED THEM OR NOT, WELL, ACTUALLY THEY WOULD KNOW IF WE HADN'T USED THEM, BUT IF WE HAD THEY WOULDN'T KNOW ABOUT IT BECAUSE THEY WOULDN'T BE HERE, AND NEITHER WOULD THE HIGHWAY.

TOLES

AND I THOUGHT THEY WOULD KNOW ALL ABOUT US, AND WE KNOW NOTHING ABOUT THEM, NOT BECAUSE WE'RE NOT AS SMART AS THEM, BUT BECAUSE WE WON'T BE HERE THEN. I DON'T MEAN WE WON'T BE HERE BECAUSE WE USED OUR NUCLEAR WEAPONS, BECAUSE WE DIDN'T, OR WON'T, UNLESS THE OTHER SIDE DOES, BUT THEY'LL KNOW IN A HUNDRED YEARS IF IT HAPPENED OR NOT.

AND TO GET TO THE POINT, IN A HUNDRED YEARS...

I'M SORRY MR. PRESIDENT, I'LL HAVE TO CUT YOU OFF, WE DON'T HAVE THAT LONG.

OH, THAT'S OKAY. I NEVER FINISHED THE LETTER, EITHER.

October 23, 1984

October 24, 1984

October 25, 1984

October 30, 1984

November 1, 1984

110

November 4, 1984

November 5, 1984

November 11, 1984

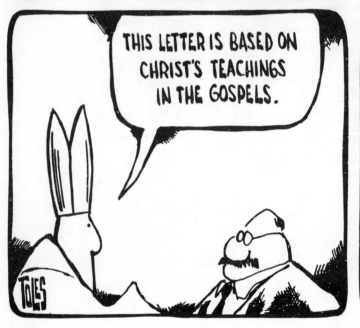

NICARAGUA SCRAPBOOK

U.S. Funds Nicaraguan Rebels

C.I.A. Mines Nicaraguan Harbors

C.I.A. Writes Nicaraguan Terrorism Handbook

U.S. Vows to Keep Pressure on Sandinistas

Administration Keeps Nicaragua Guessing About U.S. Intentions

Nicaragua Building Up Military at Increased Rate

U.S. Surprised, Indignant

Administration Keeps U.S. Public Guessing About U.S. Intentions

TOLES

118

Another Episode of General's Hospital

YOU'LL REMEMBER LAST TIME THE GENERAL WAS ANSWERING CRITICISM FOR SPENDING $7,622 ON A 10-CUP COFFEEMAKER.

TODAY THERE WAS A NEW TOPIC.

NEW TOPIC

IT WAS AN EXCITING NEW CONCEPT FOR LONGER NUCLEAR WARS.

UNDERGROUND MISSILE COMMAND CENTER

AFTER THE REGULAR NUCLEAR WAR IS OVER, WE WOULD TUNNEL TO THE SURFACE WITH MACHINES, THEN FIRE MORE MISSILES.

BEING UNDERGROUND LIKE THIS WE WON'T BE DEAD LIKE EVERYBODY ELSE, ENABLING US TO KEEP FIRING MISSILES FOR WEEKS OR EVEN MONTHS.

ISOLATION BOOTH

TOLES

JUST A COUPLE LITTLE QUESTIONS, GENERAL.

GENERAL?

...BUT THE GENERAL HAD DRIFTED OFF INTO A REVERIE

JUST LET SOMEBODY TRY AND ATTACK US NOW

CRITICS TODAY ATTACKED THE AIR FORCE FOR SPENDING $927 FOR A PLASTIC COFFEE SPOON

Launch

THAT'S BEVERAGE MODULATOR.

November 25, 1984

December 2, 1984

123

December 3, 1984

December 5, 1984

December 9, 1984

'Twas the night before Christmas, and nobody spoke,

Our Washington Santa was finally broke.

Supply-side was nestled all warm in his bed,

But visions of balance were all in his head.

FEDERAL BUDGET

'Twas time to decide about Christmas this year,

DEC. 24

He looked in his sack and said I'M STAYING HERE.

The cookies and milk all set out as a treat,

He decided to go. I STILL GOTTA EAT.

AND HE SAID AS THE COOKIES ALL VANISHED FROM SIGHT, MERRY CHRISTMAS TO ALL AND TO ALL A TAX BITE

TOLES

December 11, 1984